Rebuilding the BROKEN ALTARS

True Worship that Glorifies God

DOUGLAS DOE

Foreword by Pastor Dipo Oluyomi

Copyright © Douglas Doe, 2012

All rights reserved. The reproduction of any part of this material in any form is prohibited unless prior permission has been sought from and given by the publisher.

Published by Douglas Doe 2012
ISBN: 978-0-9571174-0-2

Book Website: **www.brokenaltars.net**

Contact Email: **info@brokenaltars.net**

Facebook: www.facebook.com/dougydoe
Twitter: www.twitter.com/dougydoe
Google+: https://plus.google.com/u/0/
LinkedIn: http://uk.linkedin.com/pub/douglas-adisenu-doe/4/912/671

Unless otherwise stated, all scripture quotations are from *The Amplified Bible, Old Testament* Copyright © 1965, 1987 by the Zondervan Corporation. *The Amplified Bible, New Testament* Copyright © 1954, 1958, 1987 by the Lockman Foundation. Used by permission.

Scripture quotations marked New Living Translation are from the *Holy Bible, New Living Translation* Copyright © 1996, 2004. Used by the permission of Tyndale House Publishing, Inc., Wheaton, IL 60189. All rights reserved.

Scripture quotations marked Message Bible are from *The Message: The Bible in Contemporary English*, Copyright © 1993, 1994, 1995, 1996, 2000, 2001, 2002. Used by permission of NavPress Publishing Group.

Scripture quotations marked New International Version are from THE HOLY BIBLE, NEW INTERNATIONAL VERSION®, NIV® Copyright © 1973, 1978, 1984, 2011 by Biblica, Inc.™ Used by permission. All rights reserved worldwide.

Scripture quotations marked Contemporary English Version are from *Contemporary English Version®* Copyright © 1995 American Bible Society. All rights reserved.

Scripture quotations marked New Century Version are from the *New Century Version*. Copyright © 1987, 1988, 1991 by Thomas Nelson, Inc. Used by permission. All rights reserved.

Scripture quotations marked GOD'S WORD Translation is taken from *God's Word to the Nations*. Quotations are used by permission. Copyright © 1995 by God's Word to the Nations. All rights reserved.

Scripture quotations marked KJV is taken from the King James Version of the Bible.

Acknowledgements

○ ○ ○

I would like to express my heartfelt thanks to my Lord and Saviour; Jesus Christ, for planting in me the initial seed to write this book and for the strength and grace to bring it to fruition. I truly owe you my life and everything your grace has enabled me to become.

To my lovely wife, Julia, thanks for all the support and encouragement you gave me in completing this assignment. Your editorial and creative expertise has contributed to making this book what it is. You are the sweetest and the best. I love you.

My profound gratitude goes to Pastor Matthew Ashimolowo, Senior Pastor of Kingsway International Christian Centre, for your inspiring and prophetic messages that have kept this dream alive. You've always encouraged us to be the best and to make a difference in our generation. This is a fruit of your messages.

A special thanks to Pastor Dipo Oluyomi, CEO of Kingsway International Christian Centre, UK, for taking the time to review the manuscript and writing the foreword. Your uncompromising messages have always spurred me on to walk in the light of God's word.

To Rev. Jennifer Wallace, I say a big thank you for taking the time to write such a thorough, insightful review in spite of your busy schedule. Your passion to see women take their rightful place in society and your evangelistic missions has always been an inspiration to me.

I would also like to say a big thank you to Bishop Samuel Fuah, for taking the time to review the book. You instilled in me the passion for prayer and the pursuit of God several years ago. Your labour of love has not been in vain.

Finally, to my closest friend, Rev. Tom Bright-Davies, thank you so much for your influence and support in the area of Worship and Music over the years. You are a true friend.

Foreword

○ ○ ○

Worship is not about the song. Worship is not about the music and surely it is not about how fast or slow a song is. It is the attitude of the heart towards God. It is a lifestyle and can be lived anywhere you are in the world.

You can worship in the prison. You can worship in the office. You can worship even with your mouth gagged. It is about giving God his worth and letting him know that he is the centre of your life. It expresses itself in your thoughts, your words and indeed your actions.

The first passage in the scripture where the word **worship** was used is in **Genesis 22:5**:

> *"And Abraham said unto his young men, Abide ye here with the ass; and I and the lad will go yonder and worship, and come again to you."* **KJV**

This was an act by Abraham to go and sacrifice the best thing he had to God and he called it worship. This was his long awaited son and the hope of his legacy and fulfillment of the promise made to him by God. Now God calls him and tells him to sacrifice and lay down that future for him, even though God gave him the promise after 25 years of waiting for it.

Indeed worship is about laying down our all. Then the song to express it will follow. The music then becomes a vehicle to give it meaning.

Douglas Doe; an experienced worship leader has written this concise, straight to the point, easy to read and well researched book on worship.

I pray it fires up the readers to live a lifestyle of true worship in its ramifications.

Pastor Dipo Oluyomi
CEO, KICC U.K. and Resident Pastor, KICC South-West London

Reviews

○ ○ ○

“In every generation, God always has an agenda to execute. He reveals his plans to men and women with a burden to declare them to his people so that no one is caught unprepared when they begin to unfold. God used people like Noah, Abraham, Moses, Deborah, David and Paul to alert their generations of what He had in store.

This trend has not changed. God continues to communicate his impending agenda to ensure man is ultimately blessed when they manifest. It is in this spirit that this book, *Rebuilding the Broken Altars*, speaks.

In this book, Douglas presents the wider concept of worship and its larger purpose to us in a language anyone can understand. We are taken back to aspects of our lives in relation to God where we have failed to build or have left unattended our altars, and therefore find them in ruins. Thankfully, this book informs us that our present challenges are not peculiar to our time and it provides solutions from a biblical perspective.

Douglas Doe examines biblical truths in relation to altars, sacrifice, music, corporate worship, fruitfulness, developing a true love for God, tithing and many more concepts of Christian living and ties them into biblical worship in a way which we might have never thought related.

This book will reposition you to enable you walk in the reality of God's promises if you are diligent enough to practice the principles in it.”

Rev Tom Bright-Davies
President and Founder, Tom Bright-Davies Ministries, Ghana

"For the past few years, the Lord has been speaking to me about 'Rebuilding the Tabernacle of David,' therefore, Douglas Doe's book, *Rebuilding The Broken Altars*, comes both as a breath of fresh air and a confirmation of what I believe the Spirit of God is saying to the Body of Christ in these last days.

The issue of worship is critical to the Church because it is the pivot and platform upon which our relationship and walk with God revolves and evolves. The men and women of old, who made such an impact on the world, truly understood this and worshipped God in spirit and truth, as expressed in the ancient hymns we still sing today. Unfortunately, our lack of understanding has resulted in shallow, self-focused and self-indulged worship, as expressed by our lifestyles, as well as many of our songs.

Rebuilding The Broken Altars addresses and challenges the current definition and interpretation of worship and re-aligns it with biblical truth. Douglas has captured an essential truth and expressed it with clarity and simplicity, making the book not only enjoyable to read but also easy to understand. *Rebuilding The Broken Altars* invites us to shift our focus back to God and His prescribed terms for personal and corporate worship. Reading the book must challenge us to connect with God in a deeper, more personal, intimate and sincere way.

The message that *Rebuilding The Broken Altars* contains is both timely and urgent, and must be read by all church leaders, worship leaders and believers, not just those who are serious about worship or revival. Indeed, the privilege will be ours to heed the message Douglas has delivered in this book, as that is the only way we can be used by God to effectively impact, influence and change our world through the Gospel of Jesus Christ."

Rev Jennifer Abigail Wallace
Executive Director, Women in Tune
A Sub-ministry of CEDARS HOUSE CHRISTIAN (INTERNATIONAL)

"As Christians the essence of our very existence is to render to God absolute Worship.

In the book *Rebuilding the Broken Altars*, there is a call back to the place of intimacy with God through True Worship. I highly recommend this book and believe this book will impact countless numbers of lives around the Globe."

Bishop Samuel C. Fuah
Founder, World Prayer Centre, Baltimore, Maryland

Contents

○ ○ ○

INTRODUCTION 1

CHAPTER ONE
Worship – What Is It? 5

CHAPTER TWO
Worship – The Significance of Altars 19

CHAPTER THREE
Worship – An Activity or a Lifestyle? 29

CHAPTER FOUR
Worship – The Key to a Fruitful Life 41

CHAPTER FIVE
Worship – What Has Money Got To Do With It? 55

Worship Nuggets 69

About the Author 71

○ ○ ○

INTRODUCTION

Introduction

○ ○ ○

As we draw close to the end of the age and the second coming of our Lord Jesus Christ, I believe we are going to see the dramatic fulfilment of Bible prophecy. There will be wars and rumours of wars, there will be famine and iniquity will abound. For those living in Europe especially, the severe economic storm engulfing the continent coupled with the prospect of the emergence of a single government is the clearest indication that the arrival of the Anti-Christ is around the corner.

In the midst of all these negatives, I also believe that we will see the greatest outpouring of God's spirit the world has ever known; to bring in the end-time harvest of souls before our Lord and Saviour Jesus Christ returns. There is coming a revival – a spiritual and financial revival to complete the task of bringing in the end-time harvest.

Before this revival however, God will prepare his people. There must be a return of his glorious church to his ways. There will be a remnant who will fear no one and nothing but the Lord.

One of the things God will restore in these seasons of preparation will be "true worship". I say true worship because there is a lot of misconception about what true worship is. Some believe it is playing high tempo music and dancing to it. Some also believe it entails singing "Christian" songs along with the waving or raising of hands. Others also believe it is just part of the programme during a Sunday service where music is played along with singing before the Preacher takes over.

Undoubtedly, music plays a very crucial role in our worship lives either individually or corporately in our congregations but all the above definitions or interpretations of worship are far from the truth.

INTRODUCTION

In seasons of preparation, God reveals his intentions to his people and one of the ways he does this is through the prophetic. Indeed, **Amos 3:7** declares that God will do nothing without first revealing it to his servants the prophets.

Elijah, in my opinion, was one of the most unique prophets of Israel. His ministry was characterised by great signs and wonders. Some of the unique occurrences in his ministry are listed below:

- He was caught up into heaven without tasting death physically. **II Kings 2:11**
- He appeared on the mount of transfiguration alongside Jesus and Moses. **Luke 9:30-31**
- John the Baptist came in the Spirit of Elijah. **Malachi 4:5-6**
- He is believed to be one of the two witnesses referred to in. **Rev 11:3-12**

His significance in the dealings and workings of God throughout the scriptures cannot be over emphasised. Yet, before challenging the Prophets of Baal on Mount Carmel's miraculous event that ushered in his public ministry, he did something extremely significant. The bible declares that:

> "*...he **repaired** the [old] **altar** of the Lord that had **been** broken down [by Jezebel].*" **I Kings 18:30**

In other words, before he initiated one of the greatest revivals in his day, he 'prepared' himself by rebuilding the BROKEN ALTARS. This resulted in:

- The destruction of all the prophets of Baal (symbolic of sin, darkness and idolatry).

- The people declaring with one voice that ... *The Lord, he is God; The Lord, he is God* (symbolic of worship).
- The opening of the heavens after three and a half years for rain (symbolic of revival and restoration) to come down.

Zachariah emphasised the importance of worship preceding any move of God by declaring that when we fail to worship the Lord of Host, there will be no rain. **Zachariah 14:17**

My prayer is that the thoughts in this book will motivate you to become part of the remnant of true worshipers who will usher in this move of God.

The world is waiting for the manifestation of the sons of God. The evidence of transformed lives is what will convince them to stop and take notice. They want to see substance and not pretence. Understanding true worship and the commitment to walk in this truth is a key to experiencing this move of God.

As the lifestyle of worship becomes our passion, we will truly set the stage for God to invade our lives and see him draw many to his knowledge.

> *"And I, if and when I am lifted up from the earth [on the cross], will draw and attract all men [Gentiles as well as Jews] to Myself."*
> **John 12:32**

CHAPTER ONE

○ ○ ○

Worship – What Is It?

Worship – What Is It?

○ ○ ○

The concept of worship is very prevalent throughout religion in general. The word is derived from the Old English **worthscipe**, meaning worthiness or worth-ship — to give, at its simplest, worth to something. This usually relates to a response from us humans to a deity.

As far as the nation of Israel was concerned, worship usually meant the observation of certain rituals which God had prescribed in his laws to express their devotion to Him. Where this devotion is directed towards any other person or god, it becomes idolatry.

A study of the word **'worship'** and how it is used in the New Testament especially, reveals the following interesting facts:

Worship or **worshipped** appears about 250 times in the King James Version of the Bible.

- It was first mentioned in Genesis 22:5 when Abraham inferred to the apparent sacrifice of his son Isaac as an act of worship.
- There are 13 Greek words used 80 times in the New Testament to refer to worship.
- Out of these 13 words, one word **proskyneo** (pronounced *pros-koo-neh'-o)* is used 60 times. The Hebrew equivalent is **shachah** (pronounced *shaw-khaw'*)
- **proskyneo** literally means to "lean towards or bow (pro) and kiss the hand (kyneo)". Generally referring to a physical gesture or posture of homage such as prostrating oneself in an expression of profound reverence.

- It is interesting to note that out of the 80 occurrences of these 13 words in the New Testament, only 3 times does it infer to the use of music or singing.
- Also interesting is the fact that, **proskyneo** is only mentioned once in reference to an assembly in **I Corinthians 14:25**. This fact, in my opinion, seems to negate the idea that a group of people must be seen to be engaged in a form of a 'religious' activity like singing or dancing for worship to have occurred.
- The word that ranks second in the number of occurrences is **sebomai** (6 times and pronounced *seb'-om-ahee*) which means to "revere, awe or to venerate" and the third is **latreuo** (4 times and pronounced *lat-ryoo'-o*) meaning to "serve in a priestly and, or sacrificial manner".
- Whenever the word **proskyneo** is used in reference to a man physically gesturing towards another man, it is translated **"bow down"**. However, when it is used in reference to a physical gesture towards God, it's translated **"worship"**.

So, does a mere physical gesture such as bowing down, kneeling, raising of hands, clapping of hands, dancing or building an altar implies we have **'sebomai'** or **'latreuo'** God? Shouldn't there be an underlying heart condition to all these physical expressions to make them acceptable sacrifices before God?

Lets us walk through the key scripture verses that this book is based on to discover what God has to say about true worship.

> *Then Elijah said to all the people, come near to me. And all the people came near him. And he repaired the [old] altar of the Lord that had been broken down [by Jezebel].*

> *Then Elijah took twelve stones, according to the number of the tribes of the sons of Jacob, to whom the word of the Lord came, saying, Israel shall be your name.*
>
> *And with the stones Elijah built an altar in the name [and self-revelation] of the Lord. He made a trench about the altar as great as would contain two measures of seed…*
>
> *Then the fire of the Lord fell and consumed the burnt sacrifice and the wood and the stone and the dust, and also licked up the water that was in the trench.*
>
> *When all the people saw it, they fell on their faces and they said, The Lord, He is God! The Lord, He is God!*
>
> *And Elijah said, seize the prophets of Baal; let not one escape. They seized them, and Elijah brought them down to the brook Kishon, and [as God's law required] slew them.*
> **I Kings 18:30-32, 38-40**

The above portion of scripture refers to an era in the history of Israel when they had departed from the Lord and his ways. Even though Ahab was the King at the time, he allowed his wife to undermine his authority and as a result she instituted Baal (idol) worship, clearly ignoring the instructions of the Lord.

Meanwhile, Elijah had declared that there would be no rain over the land because of the evil regime that Jezebel was perpetuating. After three and half years of drought, it was time for Israel to decide who their God was; was it Baal or Jehovah?

Elijah went to King Ahab and demanded that he gather all the prophets of Baal at Mount Carmel for a showdown. Elijah slaughtered two bulls and placed them on an altar. The prophets of Baal would call on their god and he would also call on Jehovah. The one who answered by fire would be the True God of Israel.

As expected, Baal never showed up all day as his prophets called on him. When the **time for offering the evening sacrifice** came, Elijah did something quite significant before calling on Jehovah. The bible says that:

> "*...and he repaired the [old] altar of the Lord that had been broken down [by Jezebel].*" I Kings 18:30

An altar is a place of sacrifice or death, which is symbolic of worship or the giving up of everything for the pursuit of the Lord. In Old Testament days, when the Israelites were ready to worship God, they had to build an altar and offer a sacrifice and God inevitably responded provided his conditions were met, and in this case by fire.

> "*Then Elijah took twelve stones, according to the number of the tribes of the sons of Jacob, to whom the word of the Lord came, saying, Israel shall be your name...*" I Kings 18:31-32

Notice what Elijah used; twelve stones symbolic of the twelve sons of Jacob who later became known as Israel, representing the foundation of the Nation of Israel. In other words, he built the right foundation by repenting on behalf of all the 12 tribes of Israel before calling on the Name of the Lord.

In today's spiritual Israel (i.e. the Church of Jesus Christ), our HEARTS are symbolic of the ALTAR. Our affections must continually be guarded so that nothing takes the place of God. Therefore, the "sacrifice" that must constantly be laid on the "altar" of our hearts must be a giving away of ourselves to God which is what worship is really about. Jesus said the first and most important commandment is this:

> *"And you shall love the Lord Your God out of and with your whole heart and out of and with all your soul (your life) and out of and with all your mind (your faculty of thought and your moral understanding) and out of and with all your strength. This is the first and principal commandment."* **Mark 12:30**

What then is true worship? I believe understanding what true worship is and pursuing it passionately is at the heart of our calling and what is foremost on God's heart.

Paul's passionate plea to the church in Rome was this:

> *"I appeal to you therefore, brethren, and beg of you in view of [all] the mercies of God, to make a decisive dedication of your bodies [presenting all your members and faculties] as a living sacrifice, holy [devoted, consecrated] and well pleasing to God, which is your reasonable [rational, intelligent] service and* **spiritual worship.***"* **Romans 12:1**

According to the above scripture, yielding all that we have and are, is equal to spiritual worship. Is there any difference between this statement in Rom 12:1 and what Jesus said in Mark 12:30? I don't think so.

Growing up as a young believer, I assumed that praise and worship was just limited to that segment in a church service where we clapped our hands and danced to exuberant music.

Even though the Bible has a lot to say about the role music plays in the expression of our praise and worship, true worship goes far beyond just music. As we saw earlier, only 3 times does the word **worship** infer to music or singing in the New Testament. In fact, it is only when our lives become a reflection of a true worshiper that music, used as a medium of expressing our worship becomes meaningful and ultimately, an acceptable sacrifice to the Lord. (We'll have more to say about the role of music in subsequent chapters).

Even though our emphasis is on worship in this book I will attempt to bring a distinction between praise and worship before proceeding further.

Praise is a response of gratitude from us to God for the things he has done or is doing in our lives or in creation as a whole. Let's take a look at a few scriptures to emphasise this point.

> *Praise the Lord! Praise God in His sanctuary; praise Him in the heavens of His power! Praise Him for His might acts; praise Him according to the abundance of His greatness!* **Psalm 150:1-2**

In this psalm, we are encouraged to praise him FOR his might acts and FOR his abundant greatness.

> *Praise the Lord! Praise the Lord from the heavens, praise Him in the heights! Praise Him, all His angels, Praise Him, all His hosts! Praise Him, sun and moon, Praise Him, all you stars of light!* **Psalm 148:1-3**

Here, the whole of creation is being admonished to praise the Lord and not just us humans.

> *Enter his gates with thanksgiving and a thank offering and into His courts with praise! Be thankful and say so to Him, bless and affectionately praise His name!* **Psalm 100:4**

Again we are admonished approach the Lord with a thankful heart and to always maintain a grateful heart in appreciation for what He has done.

Worship goes a step further than that. It is our response to God for who he is and the least we can do is to yield our entire lives unreservedly to him for no other reason than the fact that he is God. In other words, while praise is based on the **Acts** of God, we worship him because of his **Character**.

It is important therefore, to understand some of the Names of God as revealed in the scriptures since God's names are essentially a revelation of his character or who he is.

ELOHIM

It's the name that demonstrates his creative power, authority, dominion, and glory.

> "*In the beginning GOD (prepared, formed, fashioned, and) created the heavens and the earth.*" **Genesis 1:1**

JEHOVAH

In Jehovah, he is our personal God who is always with us. We can have a relationship with Him.

> "*Then the Lord God formed man from the dust of the ground and breathed into his nostrils the breath or spirit of life, and man became a living being.*" **Genesis 2:7**

JEHOVAH EL SHADDAI

◯

The Almighty God who is more than enough for me.

> *When Abram was ninety-nine years old, the Lord appeared to him and said, I am the Almighty God; walk and live habitually before Me and be perfect (blameless, wholehearted, complete).*
Genesis: 17:1

JEHOVAH ADONAI

◯

God becomes my Master, Ruler and Lord.

> *And said, My Lord if now I have found favour in your sight, do not pass by your servant, I beg of you.* **Genesis 18: 3**

JEHOVAH JIREH

◯

The Lord who sees ahead and makes provision for me.

> *So Abraham called the name of that place; The Lord Will Provide. And it is said to this day; on the mount of the Lord it will be provided.* **Genesis 22:14**

JEHOVAH ROPHE

◯

The Lord my healer.

> *…Saying, If you will diligently hearken to the voice of the Lord your God and will do what is right in His sight, and will listen to and obey His commandments and keep all His statutes, I will*

put none of the diseases upon you which I brought upon the Egyptians, for I'm the Lord Who heals you." **Exodus 15:26**

JEHOVAH NISSI

The Lord my Banner or Victor.

"*And Moses built an altar and called the name of it; The Lord is my Banner;*" **Exodus: 17:15**

JEHOVAH M'KADDESH

The Lord my Sanctifier.

"*Say to the Israelites, Truly you shall keep My Sabbaths, for it is a sign between Me and you throughout your generations, that you may know that I, The Lord, sanctify you [set you apart for Myself].*" **Exodus 31:13**

JEHOVAH SHALOM

The Lord my Peace.

"*Then Gideon built an altar there to the Lord and called it, The Lord is Peace…*" **Judges 6:24a**

JEHOVAH TSIDKENU

The Lord my Righteousness.

"*In His days Judah shall be saved and Israel shall dwell safely:*

and this is His name by which He shall be called: The Lord Our Righteousness. **Jeremiah 23:6, 33:16**

JEHOVAH ROHI

The Lord my shepherd.

The Lord is my Shepherd [to feed, guide, and shield me], I shall not lack. **Psalm 23:1**

JEHOVAH SHAMMAH

The Lord is there or the every present God.

The distance around the city shall be 18,000 [4 [4,500] measures; and the name of the city from that day and ever after shall be THE LORD IS THERE. **Ezekiel 48:35**

Now, because we (born-again believers) are reconciled to God through the Blood of Jesus, God has become all the above to us. What else can we desire than for God to manifest all these aspects of himself in and through us?

Our response must be one of absolute surrender to him and to his purposes. Our heart's cry must be that "Lord, even if you do not do anything else for us, you are too awesome and you deserve the adoration for everything that we have become. You didn't have to die for us but you did. You didn't have to create us because you are sufficient by yourself, but you chose to create us so we can give you pleasure".

You are worthy, O Lord our God, to receive glory and honour and power. For you created everything, and it is for your pleasure

> *that they exist and were created."* Revelation 4:11 [New Living Translation]

His greatness is unsearchable, his wisdom is infinite, and His power and abilities are matchless.

It is very naive for us believers to assume that just coming into a church service or a Christian gathering, raising up hands and singing Christian or "worship" songs constitutes worship. How wrong!!! Infact, when we lift up our hands during our corporate gatherings or devotional times in worship expression, it isn't meant to be a religious exercise. Rather, it should symbolise the utter surrender of our hearts to God sacrificially. King David reinforces this assertion in the Psalms:

> "*….the lifting up of my hands **as** the evening sacrifice.*" Psalm 141:2

The following statements define perfectly what I believe the heart of worship is from God's perspective.

- True worship is an attitude of the heart or a lifestyle that is totally yielded to the Lord Jesus in absolute obedience to him and his word.
- It is a life of whole-hearted, sincere and pure devotion to the Lord Jesus.
- It is a heart attitude of awe and reverence, where the overwhelming desire is to do and submit to the will of God, in whatever form or shape by the help and Grace of God.
- This unconditional devotion to God is not based on anything that the Lord has done or will do, but simply based on who God Is.
- It is having the right motives behind what we do i.e., the heart behind our actions must be right.

Our times of worship in our church services must actually be a *true expression* of our on-going day-to-day life of obedience and devotion and not an end in itself. If this is the case, then our expression of worship becomes powerful and meaningful and it ascends unto the Lord as sweet incense and a memorial before him.

God will then have no option but to show up in this kind of atmosphere just like he did in the case of Elijah and consumed the sacrifice and leaked the water under the stones because the broken altar was rebuilt. Glory to God!

True worship will cause the impossible to be possible because God Almighty will show up.

> *But You are holy, O You Who dwell in [the holy place where] the praises of Israel [are offered].* **Psalm 22:3**

What is the point in lifting up "holy hands" and singing a song about love to the Lord when we do not obey his word? In reality, we are mocking ourselves and our offering at that point becomes what the bible describes as **"strange fire"** unto the Lord.

> *And Nadab and Abihu, the sons of Aaron, each took his censer and put fire in it, and put incense on it, and offered* **strange** *and* **unholy** *fire before the Lord, as He has not commanded them. And there came forth fire from before the Lord and killed them, and they died before the Lord. Then Moses said to Aaron, This is what the Lord meant when He said, I [and my will, not their own] will be acknowledged as hallowed by those who come near Me, and before all the people I will be honoured. And Aaron said nothing.* **Leviticus 10:1-3**

> *"If you [really] love me, you will keep (obey) my commands."*
> **John 14:15**

As you can see from the scripture in Leviticus, the result of offering strange fire and incense (symbolic of worship) before the Lord can be very disastrous.

I believe it is time we return to that place where we rebuild altars of true worship with our lives because God is still looking for true worshippers who will worship him in spirit and in truth (**John 4:24**). The heavens will open again and the fire will come down like it did for Elijah. It doesn't matter how long the heavens have been shut, true worship will unlock them and God will be glorified again.

When we decide that come what may, Jehovah is the only God we will serve, we are setting ourselves up for the miraculous. When we truly worship in his Name, God will reveal the aspect of his Name that we need to experience in our lives.

True worship; or rebuilding the broken altars of our hearts means allowing God to transform us and remoulding our character to enable the fruit of the Spirit to shine forth in our lives.

It is more than just singing songs to the Lord. In fact, the songs we sing must be a reflection of what we really are inside and how we truly live or desire to live on a daily basis. Only then will the fire of God come down and consume all the impurities in our sacrifice and bring out the life of God through us.

CHAPTER TWO

● ● ●

Worship – The Significance of Altars

Worship – The Significance of Altars

○ ○ ○

Throughout the Bible, altars have always played a very significant role in the lives of God's chosen people.

An altar represents a place of sacrifice, a place where all is laid bare for God's fire to consume our offerings. It is important to notice that we have to build the altar and do the laying down of all, before the Lord sends down the fire. That is our responsibility and we ought to do that willingly. It is a way of saying to the Lord that *"I trust you implicitly, I believe you with all of my heart and soul, I will wait until my change comes."*

It is interesting to note that all the men God used in the Old Testament built an altar or altars at some point in their walk with God. Why was that so important? I believe it was symbolic of the surrendering of their entire lives to the call God had for them. That was a shadow or a type of what was to come in the New Testament where Jesus became the ultimate sacrifice.

> *Sacrifice and offering You do not desire, nor have You delight in them; You have given me the capacity to hear and obey [Your law, a more valuable service than] burnt offerings and sin offerings [which] You do not require. Then said I, Behold, I come; in the volume of the book it is written of me; I delight to do Your will, O my Gods; yes, Your law is within my heart.* **Psalm 40:6-8, Hebrews 10:5-9**

NOAH

AFTER NOAH AND HIS FAMILY emerged from the Ark unscathed from the earth's destruction by forty days of incessant rain, the **first** thing he did was to build an altar and offer a sacrifice to the Lord. God acknowledged this offering by declaring that he would **NEVER** destroy his creation like he had done anymore.

God will always respond to true worship wherever it is offered.

> *"And Noah built an **altar** to the Lord and took of every clean [four-footed] animal and of every clean fowl or bird and offered burnt offerings on the altar. When the Lord smelled the pleasing odor [a scent of satisfaction to His heart], the Lord said to Himself, I will never again curse the ground because of man, for the imagination (the strong desire) of man's heart is evil and wicked from his youth; neither will I ever again smite and destroy every living thing, as I have done."* **Genesis 8:20-21**

ABRAHAM

GOD CALLED ABRAHAM (still called Abram at this stage), gave him loads of promises and told him to move out of Haran with his family to the land that he was going to show him. When they came to the land of Canaan, the **first** thing that Abraham also did was to build an altar to the Lord. He subsequently went on to build other altars at different stages in his walk with God.

> *Then the Lord appeared to Abram and said, I will give this land to your posterity. So Abram built an **altar** to the Lord, Who had appeared to him.* Genesis 12:7

> *After that, Abram travelled southward and set up camp in the hill country between Bethel on the west and Ai on the east. There he built an **altar** and worshiped the Lord.* Genesis 12:8 [New Living Translation]

> *This was the place where Abram had built the **altar**, and there he again **worshiped** the Lord.* Genesis 13:4 [New Living Translation]

> *Then Abram moved his camp to the oak grove owned by Mamre, which is at Hebron. There he built an **altar** to the Lord.* Genesis 13:8 [New Living Translation]

> *When they arrived at the place where God had told Abraham to go, he built an **altar** and placed the wood on it..* Genesis 22:9a [New Living Translation]

ISAAC

THE LORD APPEARED TO HIM in the Land of Gerar when a severe famine had hit the land and told him not to move to Egypt (symbolic of bondage and the world system). God blessed him so much so that, the Philistines were envious of him. After a series of confrontations with the herdsmen of Gerar over his father Abraham's wells, he finally prevailed with the one he called 'Rehoboth' meaning – *The Lord has made room for us, and we shall be fruitful in the Land.*

The Lord appeared again to Isaac and renewed the covenant he had made with Abraham his father. The next action Isaac took was to build an altar unto the Lord and called on his name.

> *And the Lord appeared to him the same night and said; I am the God of Abraham your father. Fear not, for I am with you and will favour you with blessings and multiply your descendants for the sake of My servant Abraham. And [Isaac] built an **altar** there and **called** on the name of the Lord and pitched his tent there; and there Isaac's servants were digging a well.* **Genesis 26:24-25**

JACOB

THE STORY OF JACOB is one of troubles to triumph. After deceiving his brother Esau to receive the blessing from their father Isaac, he had to run away to work for his uncle Laban. He went on to endure almost 20 years of hard labour where his uncle cheated him out of his wages. During this period, he married two of Laban's daughters and had 11 children. When Joseph was born, he realised it was time to leave his uncle's employment and become his own man.

However, there was one thing in his past he knew he had to confront, and that was settling old scores with his brother Esau. He prayed to God for this meeting to be a smooth one and the Lord duly answered his prayers.

After this event, Jacob settled his family in the land of Succoth in Canaan. Notice that, the **first** thing he did after he settled was to build an altar to the Lord.

> *When Jacob came from Padanaram, he arrived safely and in*

> *peace at the town of Shechem, in the land of Canaan, and pitched his tents before the [enclosed] town. Then he bought the piece of land on which he had encamped from the sons of Hamor, Shechem's father, for a hundred pieces of money. There he erected an **altar** and called it El-Elohe-Israel [God, the God of Israel].*"
> **Genesis 33:18-20**

MANOAH AND HIS WIFE

THIS IS ANOTHER FASCINATING STORY that demonstrates the importance of altars. This couple were childless because Manoah's wife was barren. The "Angel of the Lord" *(usually referring to Jesus revealing himself in the Old Testament)* appeared to this barren woman one day as she was just minding her own business and declared she would have a son. Further instructions were given to her regarding how the baby was to be brought up because he would grow up to be a mighty deliverer.

When his wife told him about this visitation, Manoah was so desperate to experience that himself he prayed to God for the "Angel of the Lord" to return. The Bible says the Lord listened to the prayer of Manoah and "The Angel of the Lord" returned. Again, Manoah was not present so his wife kindly asked "The Angel of the Lord" to wait while she went to get her husband. Amazing!!! When Manoah arrived, the "Angel of the Lord" repeated the same prophecy he had given to his wife previously. The couple tried to offer a meal to the "Angel of the Lord" but he refused. Instead, He told them to present whatever offering they had to the Lord.

In obedience, they built an altar and offered up the sacrifice to the Lord. The prophetic word came to pass and Samson was born. Unfortunately, Samson's life ended in tragedy because of disobedience and indiscipline.

> *So Manoah took the kid with the cereal offering and offered it upon a rock to the Lord, the Angel working wonders, while Manoah and his wife looked on. For when the flame went up toward the heavens from the altar, the Angel of the Lord **ascended in the altar flame**. And Manoah and his wife looked on, and they fell on their faces to the ground.* **Judges 13:19-20**

Notice how the Angel of the Lord *"...ascended in the altar flame"*. In other words, God was so pleased with the offering on the altar that he consumed all of it by ascending in the flame; how powerful!! The worship offered by this couple was so sweet God had no choice but to "eat" all of it; symbolised by the fact that, worship is indeed God's food. As they saw what "The Angel of the Lord" did, they couldn't help but fall on their faces in total surrender.

We could go on and on about various individuals in the bible who built altars after encounters with the Lord.

- Moses built the altar of sacrifice (also known as the brazen altar) and the altar of Incense in the Tabernacle; **Exodus 27:1-2, 30:1, 3-4**
- Joshua built an altar unto the Lord after the destruction of Ai. **Joshua 8:30**
- Gideon built an altar after a visitation from the Lord. **Judges 6:24**
- Samuel built an altar to the Lord after a great victory over the Philistines. **I Samuel 7:17**
- Saul built an altar to the Lord when he wanted to inquire of him. **I Samuel 14:35**
- David built an altar to the Lord when he needed his intervention. **II Samuel 24:21**

The question is; why would all these men take the time to build an altar? What is so unique about altars that provoked all these men that God used to build them? I believe that was the highest form of expression as far as their worship of God was concerned. It was a way of saying to the Lord… *"with my best gift on this altar, I surrender all to you. I love you with every fibre of my being. For who you are and all you've done, following you with my very life is the least I can do. You deserve my love and obedience because you first loved me".*

Today, the altars in our lives must be the deepest part of our hearts where Jesus is truly enthroned as Lord. By saying he is Lord; the implication is that he has the final say in all we do. It is only when we get to this point that we can truly begin to see the genuine manifestation of God's grace in every area of our lives.

For God to ensure we arrive at this place, he will use trials, orchestrate circumstances and situations that will test and prove us. We may falter along the way but it is only to make us aware of the various areas we need to work on and straighten out if we have a pure motive. This is what true worship is all about.

> *"For from the rising of the sun to its setting My name shall be great among the nations, and in every place incense shall be offered to My name, and indeed a **pure offering**; for My name shall be great among the nations, says the Lord of hosts."* **Malachi 1:11**

Offerings will go up unto the Lord from nations all over the world but for God to accept them, they must be pure according to the above scripture. What is the quality of our worship? Is it pure?

Manoah and his wife wanted to honour the Lord after the prophecy was fulfilled but the Lord taught them a valuable lesson as they saw the "Angel of the Lord" ascend in the altar flame, which is this: learn to live the lifestyle of a worshiper and don't just worship when something good happens.

> ❝ *And Manoah said to the Angel of the Lord, What is your name, so that when your words come true, we may do you honor?* ❞
> **Judges 13:17**

I believe the "Angel of the Lord" was trying to get them to understand that his name is I AM. He is always the same yesterday, today and forever and that is enough reason to worship me always and not just when you experience something good.

Indeed, Habakkuk the prophet couldn't be more emphatic about this when he stated the importance of maintaining an attitude of worship regardless of our circumstance

> ❝ *Though the fig tree does not blossom and there is no fruit on the vines, [though] the product of the olive fails and the fields yield no food, though the flock is cut off from the fold and there are not cattle in the stalls, Yet I will rejoice in the Lord; I will exult in the [victorious] God of my salvation!* ❞ **Habakkuk 3:17:18**

Let us strive to give God all he wants which is true worship and he will surely manifest himself in our daily lives. He is an awesome God.

CHAPTER THREE

○ ○ ○

Worship – An Activity or a Lifestyle?

Worship – An Activity or a Lifestyle?

○ ○ ○

It is important that the believer does not get stuck into the activity syndrome. We should not be driven to "do" things for God to the extent that the motive for doing what we do is no more important. The quality of our service to the Lord will be greatest when it flows out of the depth of our relationship with him and not just for the sake of "doing something" for the Lord.

The routine of activity must never replace the number one reason why we were created, which is to know him intimately, pleasure him and make him known.

> *You are worthy, O Lord our God, to receive glory and honour and power. For you created everything, and it is for your pleasure that they exist and were created.* **Revelation 4:11 [New Living Translation]**

The prophet Isaiah also reminded the nation of Israel that unless sacrifices were offered to the Lord from a pure heart, they were in vain.

> *To what purpose is the multitude of your sacrifices to Me [unless they are the offering of the heart]? says the Lord. I have had enough of the burnt offerings of rams and the fat of fed beasts [without obedience]; and I do not delight in the blood of bulls or of lambs or of he-goats [without righteousness].* **Isaiah 1:11**

Very often we hear statements from church folks like; "Let's do some worship", "Oh! I missed the worship" or "The worship was awesome". Usually those who make such statements tend to refer to the time in our services when we **EXPRESS** our worship to the Lord. I believe that those times are important and they must be kept sacred at all times as it creates the kind of atmosphere that will allow God's spirit to fully operate in our mist and touch us. The Psalmist said:

> "*I will give great praise and thanks to the Lord with my mouth; yes, and I will praise Him among the multitude*" **Psalm 109:30**

He said again that:

> "*Praise The Lord! I will praise and give thanks to the Lord with my whole heart in the council of the upright and in the congregation.*" **Psalm 111:1**

Then In Psalm 22:3, which happens to be one of my favourite verses as far as worship and praise, is concerned, he said:

> "*But You are holy, O You who dwell in [the holy place where] the praises of Israel [are offered].*" **Psalm 22:3**

It is very explicit from these verses that corporate expression of our worship is scriptural and very important for us to experience the **manifest** presence of God when we congregate together.

However, the **expressions** of our worship must not be confused or substituted with what true worship is. In fact, it is a lifestyle of worship that empowers and gives substance to our expressions and causes God's presence and power to be made manifest in unique ways. Ultimately, the greater our consecration to God, the stronger his presence and the end result is his blessing being released to us.

The extent to which we **"practice"** the **Omnipresence** of God in our daily lives determines the degree to which we experience the **Manifest Presence** of God in our corporate gatherings.

Practicing the presence of God simply means we acknowledge the fact that God is with and around us 24-hours a day, everywhere. The implication is that, the attitude of reverence and awe which we would maintain if God were to be physically present with us should be the same regardless of where we find ourselves as saints of God. Whether we are in a church service, the workplace, in the shopping mall or driving our cars; we must respect, honour and reverence his presence. I believe having a clear revelation of this concept of walking with God and being committed to practicing it will dramatically change our lives and make us worthy ambassadors for God's kingdom.

It will influence the way we conduct ourselves wherever we are and how we treat people because we are always conscious of His presence and desiring to please Him.

True Worship is **not** an "event" that takes place for 30 minutes during a church service. It is a **Lifestyle**.

When worship is a lifestyle, reflecting a true heart condition that is always desiring to obey the Lord through valley or mountain top experiences, we will experience God's favour in the very minute details of our lives or in the big things. When this is our true heart condition, God's eyes will always be on us and he will accept any sacrifice of expression such as a song, or just to say to him…, "Lord I love you" because that is the truth we live and not just rhetoric .

> *A new heart will I give you and a new spirit will I put within you, and I will take away the stony heart out of your flesh and give you a heart of flesh. And I will put my Spirit within you and cause you to walk in my statutes, and you shall heed My ordinances and do them.* **Ezekiel 37:26-27**

> *For the eyes of the Lord run to and fro throughout the whole earth to show Himself strong in behalf of those whose hearts are blameless toward Him…* **II Chronicles 16:9a**

It is my fervent believe that a lifestyle of worship is the beginning of true fruitfulness in the believer's life. This may not be apparent immediately as a lot of work is done deeply in the heart by the Holy Spirit. But in time, fruits will be evident in every area of the worshipers' life.

Music and Worship

MUSIC PLAYS A VERY CRUCIAL ROLE in the life of a worshiper. God Almighty is the originator and creator of Music and he placed this inside an archangel called Lucifer (now known as satan). He was to use this solely in expressing worship to the King of Kings together with the rest of the angelic host. Since his rebellion and consequent overthrow from heaven, he has perverted this beautiful tool and music is now one of the strongest weapons he uses in his (satan's) worship and also in the destruction of lives through satanic inspired and corrupt lyrics in some secular songs.

King David, the man after God's own heart, loved to worship God with music. Most of the Psalms were written by him. He was also very skilful on the musical instrument called the harp and on one occasion brought deliverance from demonic oppression to King Saul as he played under the unction of the Holy Spirit.

> *"Saul told his servants, Find me a man who plays well and bring him to me. One of the young men said, I have seen a son of Jesse the Bethlehemite who plays skilfully, a valiant man, a man of war, prudent in speech and eloquent, an attractive person; and the Lord is with him. So Saul sent messengers to Jesse and said, Send me David your son, who is with the sheep. And Jesse took a donkey loaded with bread, a skin of wine, and a kid and sent them by David his son to Saul. And David came to Saul and served him. Saul became very fond of him, and he became his armor-bearer. Saul sent to Jesse, saying; Let David remain in my service, for he pleases me. And when the evil spirit from God was upon Saul, David took a lyre and played it; so Saul was refreshed and became well, and the evil spirit left him."* **I Sam 16:17-23**

The importance that David attached to Music as far as the Temple worship was concerned was demonstrated when he appointed Song/Worship leaders, skilful instrumentalists to take care of the Temple worship. These men were trained and skilled in music for the Lord. He had 3 main Worship leaders; Asaph, Jeduthun and Heman. Their sons were all skilled musicians and together with other family members formed a mass choir.

In most Charismatic/Pentecostal Churches today in any part of the world, it is not uncommon to see Choirs or Praise Teams whose ministry is to lead God's people into his presence primarily through the medium of music.

Clearly, apart from being trained, these key worship leaders of David were anointed and called into the ministry of worship.

> *Also David and the chiefs of the host[of the Lord] **separated** to the [temple] service some of the suns of Asaph, Heman, and Jeduthun, who should prophesy [being inspired] with lyres, harps, and cymbals. The list of the musicians according to their service was:…* **I Chronicles 25:1**

> *… play skilfully [on the strings] with a loud and joyful sound* **Psalm 33:3b**

> *O Lord, our Lord, how excellent (majestic and glorious) is Your name in all the earth!* **Psalm 8:1a**

As important as music is in our worship lives, one of the key objectives in this book is to emphasise that, **music is not worship**. It is a medium ordained by God that we use in EXPRESSING our worship or praise to him.

> *Praise him WITH… Praise him WITH… Praise him WITH…* **Psalm 150:3a, 4a, 5a**

> *O Worship the Lord IN the beauty of Holiness; tremble before and reverently fear Him, all the earth* **Psalm 96:9**

If the heart of the person offering up worship through any musical media is not right with God, then no matter how skilled the instrumentalist is, no matter how sweet the voices are, no matter how emotional we get, no matter how loud we shout, no matter how hard we clap our hands, our worship becomes an abomination to the Lord and hence God will reject our "sacrifices".

In fact, the bible calls this kind of worship *'strange fire'* as we saw in the previous chapter. As it turned out, the consequences can be very disastrous if it is not checked.

> "And Nadab and Abihu, the sons of Aaron, each took his censer and put fire in it, and put incense on it, and offered **strange** and **unholy** fire before the Lord, as He had not commanded them. And there came forth fire from before the Lord and killed them, and they died before the Lord. Then Moses said to Aaron, This is what the Lord meant when He said, I [and My will, not their own] will be acknowledged as hallowed by those who come near Me, and before all the people I will be honoured. And Aaron said nothing." **Leviticus 10:1-3**

Another version says:

> "... a different kind of fire than he had commanded..." [**New Living Translation**]

I believe we ought to give God the very best because his name is excellent. I would be the first person to advocate for excellent musical arrangements, playing skilfully and all that goes into making our music technically excellent. However, we cannot substitute true worship with just skilful music that has no unction to destroy yokes but only feeds our flesh and emotions.

When a heart is transformed by the Spirit of God and that life is surrendered to the will of God; that for me; is true worship in the light of God's word. When individuals are sold out to the Lord in this manner, then and only then will our musical expressions create an atmosphere where God's presence can come down and dwell. Healings will be easy; anything is possible in such an atmosphere.

> "But You are holy, O You Who dwell in [the holy place where] the praises of Israel [are offered]." **Psalm 22:3**

When such a heart condition exists in our lives, then the fruit of our lips through a song, a shout, playing of an instrument or a dance becomes a powerful weapon that triggers the supernatural of God on our behalf.

> *Through Him, therefore, let us constantly and at all times offer up to God a sacrifice of praise, which is the fruit of lips that thankfully acknowledge and confess and glorify His name.*
> **Hebrews 13:15**

Approaching God's presence corporately

IT IS IMPERATIVE FOR US to know and recognise that if anything is worthwhile giving to the Lord, then it must be the very best. Members in our worship teams must recognise what an awesome responsibility this is and how God must be approached with all reverence and humility. Our emphasis must be on lives that are transformed with proven character and not just people with talents who live carnal and hypocritical lifestyles. The fact is that the more yielded we are to the Lord, the more we will see his glory manifest.

We should endeavour to approach each service or the gathering of God's people with the kind of respect due God and his presence. Worship leaders must always be sensitive to sense the "mood of the Spirit". By implication, they should be able to determine if the atmosphere should be jubilant or solemn? What attribute of God should his people focus on at a particular point in time? Are we in tune with the Father of the house (the Pastor) as far as his focus and passion for that season is concerned? Any song will just not do even though it may be a "nice" worship song.

For instance, the Worship leader or the Choir may have rehearsed a particular song to minister but during the course of the worship service, the Spirit of God may be indicating a different direction and this may mean a change of song altogether. Sensitivity is the key and this is so important because the rest of the service may depend on our willingness to follow the leading of the Spirit of God in this direction. That is why the bible encourages us to:

> "*Herald and preach the Word! Keep your sense of urgency [stand by, be at hand and ready], whether the opportunity seems to be favourable or unfavourable....*" II Timothy 4:2a

Just because a Choir has rehearsed a particular song to minister in a worship service does not mean they must minister that song at all cost. This is God's business and his Spirit must be allowed to have his way fully. Within the time frame that we have in a service, it is important to cooperate fully with the Holy Spirit to maximize that time in his presence.

It is not uncommon to see believers spend hours in corporate prayer but very rarely do we spend the same quality of time just loving on God and expressing our love for him. I believe in the power of prayer and a consistent prayer life should be part and parcel of a worshiper's lifestyle. However, I also believe that worship is a higher form of prayer in that, true worship expression brings us right into the very presence of God and what is it that can stand in the Presence of the Almighty?

○

One aspect of true worship expression is really a proclamation of what God says about himself in his Word and declaring that back to him through various media such as poems, music and even silence. Yes, there are times when we just need to be silent when we are in his presence so that he may give us direction and answers to prayers we have offered to him in times past. That is why it is a higher form of prayer; when we hear and listen to his voice in the secret place and not just making requests all the time.

King David summarised this perfectly in the following Psalm when he said:

> *One thing have I asked of the Lord, that will I seek, inquire for, and [insistently] require: that I may dwell in the house of the Lord [in His presence] all the days of my life, to behold and gaze upon the beauty [the sweet attractiveness and the delightful loveliness] of the Lord and to meditate, consider, and inquire in His temple.* **Psalm 27:4**

After King Solomon extravagantly worshiped the Lord with an uncountable number of sheep and oxen, The Bible tells us the glory of God was so strong that the priests could not stand to minister anymore.

> *King Solomon and all the congregation of Israel who had assembled before him were with him before the ark, sacrificing sheep and oxen, so many that they could not be reported or counted. And the priests brought the ark of the covenant of the Lord to its place in the Holy of Holies of the house, under the wings of the cherubim. For the cherubim spread forth their two wings over the place of the ark, and the cherubim covered the ark and its poles. The poles were so long that the ends of them were seen from the Holy Place before the Holy of Holies, but they were not seen outside; they are there to this day. There was nothing*

in the ark except two tables of stone which Moses put there at Horeb, where the Lord made a covenant with the Israelites when they came out of the land of Egypt. When the priests had come out of the Holy Place, the cloud filled the Lord's house, So the priests could not stand to minister because of the cloud, for the glory of the Lord had filled the Lord's house. " **I Kings 8:5-11**

Only heaven can reveal the blessings we may be missing by rushing in and out of God's presence and treating his presence with dishonour!

The worshiper's lifestyle must be so intimate with the Lord that the Holy Spirit becomes their only source of inspiration. If hard rock music, which has its inspiration from Satan, can negatively influence the lives of unbelievers because of the atmosphere that it creates, then surely, anointed music must also create the kind of atmosphere that draws people to the Lord and transforms their lives.

CHAPTER FOUR

● ● ●

Worship – The Key to a Fruitful Life

Worship – The Key to a Fruitful Life

○ ○ ○

The song writers Wayne and Cathy Perrin, in a song of worship had this to say; *"All things that surround me become shadows in the light of you"*. These words encapsulate what true worship accomplishes. God is so magnified that everything just pales into insignificance. All the mountains in our lives, the problems we thought would never go away just becomes like a drop in the ocean. Our immediate circumstances may not have changed yet, but in the light of God's presence, we get a revelation of the might and awesome power of God that completely overwhelms our problems, fears, anxieties and worries. Suddenly, our faith in God becomes so energised and quickened we feel we can move every mountain and cast it into the sea.

Isaiah heard the Lord say this as he declared in prophecy:

> *"For thus says the high and lofty One—He who inhabits eternity, Whose name is Holy: I dwell in the high and holy place, but with him also who is of a thoroughly penitent and humble spirit, to revive the spirit of the humble and to revive the heart of the thoroughly penitent [bruised with sorrow for sin]."* **Isaiah 57:15**

When our lifestyle is one of worship, we will always see the Lord as the high and lofty one, as the one who inhabits eternity. If truly the Lord, Jehovah inhabits eternity, then every 'finite' situation will melt before him.

It is also important to notice that the Lord said he dwells there with those with a particular heart condition; the penitent and humble in spirit. Dwelling means *abiding permanently at a specific location*. A lifestyle of worship will always help us put things in proper perspective; that God will always be God and situations will always change no matter how long they may have lasted. With this vision of God constantly before us, we will always overcome and be victorious. God will lead us on from victory to victory.

God really wants us to come up higher until we see like Jesus sees. In the midst of the raging storms he was asleep and when he woke up, he was still in charge. He just spoke peace to the storm and they were stilled. What a God-Man to emulate? He is worthy!!!

The Worshiper's Attitude to Pain

ONE OF THE MOST IMPORTANT and fundamental truths we need to understand about God is that, the way he thinks and does things is absolutely different from our way of doing things.

> *For My thoughts are not your thoughts, neither are your ways My ways, says the Lord. For as the heavens are higher than the earth, so are My ways higher than your ways and My thoughts than your thoughts.* **Isaiah 55:8-9 [AMP]**

> *[This is] because the foolish thing [that has its source in God] is wiser than men, and the weak thing [that springs] from God is stronger than men* **I Corinthians 1:25 [AMP]**

Think about this for a moment:

- Why would God allow Abraham to wait for 25 years before he got the opportunity to experience the joy of fatherhood when he was supposed to be God's friend?
- Why did God allow Joseph to go through the pain of rejection and betrayal by his own brothers and Potiphar's wife?
- Why would David become a fugitive for almost 13 years, running away from Saul when all he did was to save a whole nation from an enemy?
- Why would God seemingly do a 'deal' with satan that would cause Job to suffer for no apparent reason when God himself testified that Job was the most upright man in all the earth at the time?
- Why would God allow a righteous man like Daniel to be thrown into the lion's den?
- Why did God allow Shadrach, Meshach and Abednego to be thrown in the fire when they took a stand not to compromise when everyone else was?
- Why would God allow Paul and Silas to be thrown into prison for preaching the gospel and casting out a demon in a young girl?
- Why would Jesus stay where he was for two more days when he heard that Lazarus, the man he loved; was very sick and indeed, allowed him to die as a result before he decided to go over to Bethany?
- Why would God allow his only begotten Son who was sinless to die a shameful and tragic death for the redemption of mankind?

When you relate the above examples to the character and nature of God Almighty, it doesn't appear to make sense for a good God to allow righteous or for that matter, worshipers to 'suffer' for doing his will. One would have thought God should have brought instant deliverance to those he loved. But Jesus made these profound statements in the gospel of John:

> ".....and He cleanses and repeatedly prunes every branch that continues to bear fruit, to make it bear more and richer and more excellent fruit." **John 15:2b**

> "I assure you, most solemnly I tell you, unless a grain of wheat falls into the earth and dies, it remains [just one grain; it never becomes more but lives] by itself alone. But if it dies, it produces many others and yields a rich harvest." **John 12:24**

God is more interested in his eternal purposes than our temporal discomfort. It is worth noting that, the final outcome in each of these incidents brought greater glory to the Lord than might have been otherwise.

Going through trails is painful. It is very hard on the flesh. So many questions arise in our minds and we wonder where God is. But the most important thing that God looks for when he allows us to go through trying and painful experiences is our RESPONSE. When our response is positive like that of Job's, the eventual outcome will promote his glory.

> "[I do it because, though He slay me, yet will I wait for and trust Him and] behold, …" **Job 13:15a**

The pain of the righteous will develop a genuine character and hunger for the Lord if the response is right. There will be a brokenness that will lead to an absolute dependence on God. This experience in turn will enable God to use us in greater and mightier ways than we could ever imagine. This must be the heart condition of a true worshiper and one of the ways that this is developed is through pain.

I don't know why God chooses to use trials and challenges to achieve his purposes but I do know that when we allow him to do things his way, we will never be disappointed. He knows the end from the beginning and he knows exactly what he is doing. When we can come to the place where we trust him even though we may not understand what is going on, then we truly have the heart of a worshiper.

For Shadrach, Meshach and Abednego, the turning point in their confrontation with King Nebuchadnezzar was in verse 18 of Daniel chapter 3 when they said they knew that God was able to and would deliver them. But even if he didn't, they would still not WORSHIP another god. What faith and courage we ought to emulate!!!! These were true worshipers and that is where God is calling us to.

> *If our God Whom we serve is able to deliver us from the burning fiery furnace, He will deliver us out of your hand, O king. **But if not**, let it be known to you, O king, that we will not serve your gods or worship the golden image which you have set up!*
> **Daniel 3:17-18**

You see, God always looks at the bigger picture. He is interested in the ultimate salvation of people far more than we think and he always has his eternal purposes in mind. He is sovereign and he decides to do things his own way and when we cooperate with him, the outcome is always glorious.

> *We are assured and know that [God being a partner in their labor] all things work together and are [fitting into a plan] for good to and for those who love God and are called according to [His] design and purpose.* **Romans 8:28**

> *God sent me before you to preserve for you a posterity and to continue a remnant on the earth, to save your lives by a great escape and save for you many survivors. So now it was not you who sent me here, but God; and He has made me a father to Pharaoh and lord of all his house and ruler over all the land of Egypt.* **Genesis 45:7-8**

I believe that God will allow us to go through unique experiences so we can appreciate what people go through if we ever want to bring God's deliverance to them. If we don't appreciate the pain of those we are called to deliver, we cannot qualify to bring deliverance to them because we cannot truly identify with them.

That is what intercession is all about. Even Jesus, though he was the Son of God, had to qualify to become the author of our eternal salvation by coming in the flesh and experiencing all that we will ever experience and overcoming them.

> *So even though Jesus was God's Son, he learnt obedience from the things that he suffered. In this way, God qualified him as a perfect High Priest, and he became the source of eternal salvation for all those who obey him.* **Hebrews 5: 8-9 [New Living Translation]**

Through many God-ordained or God-permitted experiences, God does a deep work of brokenness in our hearts which then becomes a foundation for us qualifying as true and genuine worshipers. Our testimony is not just mere words but that of substance as we become living proofs of God's awesome grace and mercy.

These sorts of experiences release the anointing of God on a song because it is no more just "another" song we sing but we're actually prophesying from a real experience. The spirit of God is then able to easily touch lives and bring conviction and draw them unto Himself.

How God works out his eternal purposes through pain is a mystery but the fact is that, this is one of the ways he works. When we examine the heroes of faith mentioned in Hebrews 11 and throughout history, men and women whom God used mightily have experienced what I will call "great valley experiences" at various times in their journey to destiny. I believe with all my heart that there is a brokenness and tenderness within the heart of a true worshipper that is only produced through patient endurance of the "process" of moulding that goes on in our lives. Remember, it is our **Response** that determines our level of intimacy with God and our ultimate level of promotion.

> *But He knows the way that I take [He has concern for it, appreciates, and pays attention to it]. When He has tried me, I shall come forth as refined gold [pure and luminous].* **Job 23:10**

For true worshipers, God will gather all our tears of pain and turn them into a spring (symbolic of a life giving source). Jesus said he is the living water and for those who believe in him, rivers of living water will flow out of our bellies. The quality of ministry that flows from the life of a true worshiper will always satisfy the thirsty and meet the needs of people we come into contact with.

> *Blessed (happy, fortunate, to be envied) is the man whose strength is in You, **in whose heart are the highways to Zion**. Passing through the Valley of **Weeping** (Baca), they make it a place of **springs**; the early rain also fills [the pools] with blessings. They go from strength to strength [increasing in victorious power]; each of them appears before God in Zion.* **Psalm 84:5-7**

> *There is a river whose streams shall make glad the city of God, the holy place of the tabernacles of the Most High.* **Psalm 46:4**

> *And you shall be like a watered garden and like a spring of water whose waters fail not.* **Isaiah 58:11b**

In Psalm 84 quoted above, notice that the one in whose heart are the highways to Zion (i.e. the worshiper) will allow his "valley of weeping" to become a life-giving source. They will eventually go from strength to strength in the power and in the things of God until they eventually appear before God in Zion or His presence; Hallelujah!!!.

David the Worshiper

DAVID, A MAN AFTER GOD'S OWN HEART was undoubtedly the most influential king Israel ever had. Such was his influence and his relationship with the Lord that, God swore by his holiness that his throne would be established forever.

> *His offspring shall endure forever, and his throne [shall continue] as the sun before Me. It shall be established forever as the moon, the faithful witness in the heavens.* **Psalm 89:34-37**

A few spiritual metaphors were ascribed to David. For instance:

- The Throne of David [Psalm 89:36]
- The Key of David [Rev 3:7]
- Psalm of David (He wrote about two-thirds of the Psalms).
- Jesus was referred to as the Son of David [Mark 10:47]
- The Seed of David [II Timothy 2:8]
- The City of David [I Kings 2:10]

- The House of David [**Zechariah 12:10**]
- The Tabernacle of David [**Amos 9:11-12**]

David also operated in the 3 messianic offices: **Prophet**, **King** and **Priest**.

- As a Prophet, he prophesied about the sufferings of the coming messiah in **Psalm 22**.
- As a King, he ruled over the people of Israel and led them to several victories in warfare against their enemies.
- As a Priest, he was a genuine worshiper and intercessor. This can be seen throughout the psalms mostly declaring the praises of God.

For all the spiritual metaphors ascribed to David, there was one that God specifically said he was going to restore in **THAT DAY** which I believe prophetically, referred to these last days in which we live.

> "In that day will I raise up the **tabernacle of David**, the fallen hut or booth, and close up its breaches; and I will raise up its ruins, and I will build it as in the days of old. That they may possess the remnant of Edom and of all the nations that are called by My name, says the Lord Who does this" **Amos 9:11-12**

The setup in the Tabernacle of David, as far as worship was concerned, was an organised, sophisticated structure of musicians, worship leaders and song ministers, a system which is still unparalleled in the church today. Those ministers were anointed, gifted, called and dedicated to the temple worship. Remember, David was a prolific song writer (as most of the Psalms that we read were actually songs) and a skilled instrumentalist (he played the harp or guitar to release Saul from demonic oppression) and above all, anointed of God.

> "Also David and the chiefs of the host[of the Lord] separated to the [temple] service some of the sons of Asaph, Heman, and

Jeduthun, who should prophesy [being inspired] with lyres, harps, and cymbals. The list of the musicians according to their service was: Of the sons of Asaph: Zaccur, Joseph, Nethaniah, and Ashrelah, the sons of Asaph under the direction of Asaph, who prophesied (witnessed and testified under divine inspiration) in keeping with the king's order. Of the sons of Jeduthun: Gedaliah, Zeri, Jeshaiah, Shimei, Hashabiah, and Mattithiah, six in all, under the direction of their father Jeduthun, who witnessed and prophesied under divine inspiration with the lyre in thanksgiving and praise to the Lord. Of Heman: the sons of Heman: Bukkiah, Mattaniah, Uzziel, Shebuel, Jerimoth, Hananiah, Hanani, Eliathah, Giddalti, Romamti-ezer, Joshbekashah, Mallothi, Hothir, and Mahazioth. All these where the sons of Heman the king's seer [his mediator] in the words and things of God to exalt Him; for God gave to Heman fourteen sons and three daughters; All of whom were [in the Choir] under the direction of their father for song in the house of the Lord, with cymbals, harps, and lyres, for the service of the house of God. Asaph, Jeduthun, and Heman were under the order of the king. So the number of them [who led the remainder of the 4,000], with their kinsmen who were specially trained in songs for the Lord all who were talented singers, was 288 " I Chronicles 25:1-7 [AMP]

A thorough study of the Tabernacle of David is not our focus here but the above portion of scriptures highlights how David's heart of worship led him to set up this institution of dedicated people to continually express worship to the Lord in the temple.

It is my fervent belief that the modern day Church can learn a great deal from David as far as his organisation, structure and commitment to raise a music team dedicated to offering ceaseless worship to the Lord was concerned.

The question then is; why would God seek to restore an "Old Testament" institution in these last days? I believe the answer can be found in verse 12 of Amos 9

> "...That they may **possess the remnant of Edom** and of all the nations that are called by my name says the Lord Who does this."

The Edomites are the descendants of Esau, Jacob's brother. Jacob represents the nation of Israel while Esau or Edom represents the Gentile nations. Symbolically these are the unsaved that must be possessed or won over to the Lord.

The restoration of the institutions of worship (which is what David's Tabernacle represents) should therefore be a tool to reach the lost or the unsaved. In effect, what the scripture above is saying is that, worship as a lifestyle and not an event, will be our greatest asset in winning over the lost.

Think about that for a moment. All our efforts to witness to the lost will be made much easier when our lifestyle speaks volumes about who and what we represent. We will not have to force or coerce people into accepting the message of the gospel. The way we live should do that work and that is what the Lord is restoring in these last days. The broken altars in our lives must be rebuilt again before we can see the power of God restored to make our lives living witnesses.

David was a man just like you and I. He had problems and struggled with shortcomings in his personal life. But listen to his heart when the prophet Nathan confronted him about his unconfessed sin:

> *"Create in me a clean heart, O God, and renew a right, persevering and steadfast spirit within me."* **Psalm 51:10**

> *"My sacrifice [the sacrifice acceptable] to God is a broken spirit; a broken and a contrite heart [broken down with sorrow for sin and humbly and thoroughly penitent], such O God, You will not despise."* **Psalm 51:17**

There it is! It's all about the heart and that is where true worship begins. No wonder God called him a man after his own heart. He had a worshiper's heart.

David loved God so much he was always prepared to get right with God as soon as he realised he had fallen short of His standards. And that is what God is looking for, not PERFECT PEOPLE but PERFECT HEARTS. A perfect heart is simply one that is passionate after the things of God, tender towards God and open to his will and direction.

> *"For the eyes of the Lord run to and fro throughout the whole earth to show Himself strong in the behalf of those whose hearts are blameless toward Him…"* **II Chronicles 16:9a**

When our heart is right, our actions will eventually be right because they will flow out of a pure motive, not for self but for Gods glory. Our verbal expressions of worship through song and music will be a pleasing sacrifice which the Lord will consume because they are backed by a consecrated lifestyle. Our lives will have no other choice than to be fruitful.

CHAPTER FIVE

○ ○ ○

Worship – What Has Money Got To Do With It?

Worship – What Has Money Got To Do With It?

○ ○ ○

Money has always been a touchy subject in the Church. In the past, the Church as a whole had held a philosophy of abstinence; that is, we shied away from talking openly about money as though it isn't important to God.

However, it is important to find out what God has to say about money especially as it relates to our worship lives.

Let's take a careful look at **Proverbs 3: 9-10** in various versions of the bible:

> "Honor the Lord by giving him your money and the first part of all your crops. Then you will have more grain and grapes than you will ever need." [Contemporary English Version, CEV]

> "Honor God with everything you own; give him the first and the best. Your barns will burst; your wine vats will brim over." [Message Bible, MSG]

> "Honor the Lord with your capital and sufficiency [from righteous labours] and with the firstfruits of all your income; so shall your storage places be filled with plenty, and your vats shall be overflowing with new wine." [Amplified Bible]

> "Honor the Lord with your wealth and with the first and best part of all your income. Then your barns will be full, and your vats will overflow with fresh wine." [God's Word Translation, GWT]

> *Honor the Lord with your wealth, with the firstfruits of all your crops; then your barns will be filled to overflowing, and your vats will brim over with new wine.* **[New International Version, NIV]**

It is abundantly clear from the above scriptures that God does want us to serve him with our money, wealth and everything that we own. In fact, everything we own or will ever own comes from God anyway.

> *Every good gift and every perfect (free, large, full) gift is from above; it comes down from the Father of all [that gives] light, in [the shining of] Whom there can be no variation [rising or setting] or shadow cast by His turning [as in an eclipse].* **James 1:17**

But does it mean just giving our money to God suggests an act of worship on the part of the giver? Nothing could be farther from the truth.

The different versions of the above scripture begin by saying, *"… Honor the Lord with or Honor the Lord by…"*. It is the Honor in our giving that makes all the difference. When we express our reverence or worship the Lord by giving to him (what he has blessed us with in the first place), the result will be us having more than enough and experiencing his blessing in every area of our lives. It is our heart condition at the time we give that will determine if God receives that gift or if it becomes just another religious exercise.

When the overriding reason why we give is to see God's work prosper, his servants well taken care of and an overall advancement of his Kingdom, then that gift or offering becomes a sweet smelling sacrifice which God receives and in turn releases his blessing upon our lives so we can always have more than enough to be a blessing to humanity.

Proverbs 3:9 reveals two kinds of giving: tithing and offering.

*"Honor the Lord with your **substance** and the **first fruit** of all your increase."* This is what we refer to as the Offering and the Tithe respectively.

Tithe

TITHING IS A PRINCIPLE instituted by God that goes far beyond money. In my opinion, it was established way back in the Garden of Eden when God told Adam and Eve they could eat of every fruit in the garden but not the Tree of Knowledge and of God and Evil. Symbolically, God was saying to Adam and Eve – "don't touch the first part of anything I give you. This should be separated to me but you can have the rest". In other words, the first fruits of everything that God gives us belong to him. This must not be done legalistically, but as a gesture of appreciation, love and honour to the King of Kings.

By definition, the tithe is the tenth of all our income or increase. In the Old Testament, because the Israelites were predominantly an agricultural nation, they would bring the best part of their crops or animal produce to the Lord.

Bringing these things by themselves does not constitute worship. As we've established already, worship is essentially an attitude of the heart. However, it is impossible to love without expressing it and expression will always result in giving. The bible says God so loved that he *gave* his only son. When we truly love the Lord, we cannot help but to give off ourselves and substance to him. It is the heart behind the giving that makes all the difference.

Both Cain and Abel brought an offering to the Lord in **Genesis 4:3-5**.

From the outside, they both appeared to have honoured the Lord with their offerings but obviously, the Lord saw their hearts and rejected that of Cain's and accepted Abel's.

Today, we do not literally bring crops and animals, but our money which represents our toil, sweat, energy and our very lives. God says when we fail to bring the tithe we are actually robbing him or stealing from him. Now, I don't know about you, but the last thing I want to be doing is stealing from God.

> "*Should a person rob God? But you are robbing me, You ask, 'How have we robbed you?' You have robbed me in your offerings and the tenth of your crops. So a curse is on you, because the whole nation has robbed me. Bring to the storehouse a full tenth of what you earn so there will be food in my house...*"
> **Malachi 3:8-10a [New Century Version]**

God always looks at the heart or motive behind what we do and tithing is no exception. Even though the tithe is the Lord's we shouldn't bring it to him out of duty. Instead, it should be out of a genuine desire to honour him and a recognition of the fact that he is truly Lord over our lives and everything we own. He expects us to bring it willingly.

Abraham gave a tithe of all when the Lord helped him to victory in battle. He gave a tithe of all to Melchizedek (who was a type of Christ)

> "*And blessed, praised and glorified be God Most High, Who has given your foes into your hand! And [Abram] gave him a tenth of all [he had taken].*" **Genesis 14: 20:21**

Jacob made a vow to the Lord saying he would bring him the tithe of all if he experienced God's protection.

> *Then Jacob made a vow, saying, If God will be with me and will keep me in this way that I go and will give me food to eat and clothing to wear. So that I may come again to my father's house in peace, then the Lord shall be my God; And this stone which I have set up as a pillar (monument) shall be God's house [a sacred place to me], and of all [the increase of possessions] that You give me I will give the tenth to You.* **Genesis 28:20-22**

The following scriptures further emphasises the importance of the tithe as an instrument of worship

> *Be sure to save one-tenth of all your crops each year. Take it to the place the Lord your God will choose where he is to be worshiped...* **Deuteronomy 14:22-23a [New Century Version]**

The Church has been divided long enough about the issue of the tithe. **We must move beyond debate into obedience.** These scriptures are as clear as crystal. The tithe belongs to the Lord and we must not only bring it to the storehouse (your local Church) so there will always be fresh manna to feed on but more importantly, with a heart of gratitude. When we bring the tithe to the Lord with this attitude, he promises to release his blessing upon our lives. Prosperity and success in all we do become inevitable.

Offerings

THE OFFERING IS A VOLUNTARY GIFT we are expected to bring to God in expression of our love and reverence for him for all he has done for us and for what he means to us.

In the Old Testament, anytime the Israelites appeared before the Lord, they were expected to bring an offering.

> *"Three times a year shall all your males appear before the Lord your God in the place which He chooses: at the Feast of Unleavened Bread, at the Feast of Weeks, and at the Feast of Tabernacles or Booths. **They shall not appear before the Lord empty-handed. Every man shall give as he is able, according to the blessing of the Lord your God which He has given you.**"* Deuteronomy 16:16-17

The book of Leviticus is full of numerous examples of the different type of offerings that they brought to the Lord. These include the Sin, Peace, Guilt, Grain and Burnt offering.

> *"Meanwhile, the fire on the altar must be kept burning; it must never go out. Each morning the priest will add fresh wood to the fire and arrange the daily whole **burnt offering** on it. He must then burn the fat of the peace offerings on top of this daily whole **burnt offering**."* Leviticus 6:12 [New Living Translation]

> *"These are the instructions regarding the different kinds of **peace offerings** that may be presented to the Lord."* Leviticus 7:11 [New Living Translation]

> *"These are the instructions regarding the **grain offering**. Aaron's sons must present this offering to the Lord in front of the altar."* Leviticus 6:14 [New Living Translation]

The main purpose of the Burnt, Grain and Peace offerings in particular, was to demonstrate a voluntary act of worship from the giver and an expression of their devotion and complete surrender to God.

As we have pointed out earlier, we in the church today do not need to bring crops or animals as we are not predominantly farmers. Money has become the universal medium of exchange and with that, every need can be met. The book of Ecclesiastes makes it even clearer for us to see.

> *A feast is made for laughter, wind makes life merry, and money is the answer for everything.* **Ecclesiastes 10:19 [New International Version]**

God uses our tithes and offerings to advance the work of his Kingdom much like the way Governments depend on taxes to promote development work in their respective nations. The big difference however, is that, taxes are exacted forcefully from citizens whereas God requires that we obey him willingly in our giving. There is nothing wrong in being admonished to give but when we give under pressure or reluctantly then our giving is in vain.

> *Let each one [give] as he has made up his own mind and purposed in his heart, not reluctantly or sorrowfully or under compulsion. For God loves (He takes pleasure in, prizes above other things, and is unwilling to abandon or to do without) a cheerful (joyous, "prompt to do it") giver [whose heart is in his giving].* **II Corinthians 9:7**

It is the heart condition behind our giving that God ultimately looks at and which determines how he blesses us.

Quality or Quantity?

THE QUALITY OF OUR GIVING is more important to God than the quantity because God prioritises the motive of our giving above the amount.

When we give with the right motive and heart attitude to God, it inevitably flows into extravagance and abundance. However, abundance is relative from God's perspective since He is the only one who truly knows our circumstances when we give.

Jesus commended the widow who gave only two mites over all the others who gave so much because that was all she had. Obviously, Jesus knew that because he could always discern the hearts of men.

> *And a widow who was poverty-stricken came and put in two copper mites [the smallest of coins], which together make half of a cent. And He called His disciples [to Him] and said to them, Truly and surely I tell you, this widow, [she who is] poverty-stricken, has put in more than all those contributing to the treasury. For they all threw in out of their abundance; but she, out of her deep poverty, has put in everything that she had – [even] all she had on which to live.* **Mark 12:42-44**

The fact that Jesus noticed this seemingly insignificant gesture portrays a very powerful lesson: God sees and checks the motives behind everything we do and he will ultimately promote or demote us as a result.

> *All the ways of a man are pure in his own eyes, but the Lord weighs the spirits (the thoughts and intents of the heart).* **Proverbs 16:2**

Once the quality issue in our giving is settled, the quantity aspect will be automatic. We will have no problems in lavishly giving to God or blessing his ministers when he prompts us to do so just like David did.

> *Moreover, because I have set my **affection** on the house of my God, in addition to all I have prepared for the holy house, I have a private treasure of gold and silver which I give for the house of my God: It is 3,000 talents of gold, gold of Ophir, 7,000 talents of*

> *refined silver for overlaying the walls of the house, Gold for the uses of gold, silver for the uses of silver, and for every work to be done by craftsmen. Now who will offer **willingly** to fill his hand [and consecrate it] today to the Lord [**like one consecrating himself to the priesthood**]?..... But who am I, and what are my people, that we should retain strength and be able to offer thus so willingly? For all things come from You, and out of Your own [hand] we have given You.* I Chronicles 29:3-4, 14

Notice how David compared giving to God willingly to one consecrating himself to the priesthood! That sounds like worship to me; as one of the key functions of the priest was to offer up incense before the Lord (symbolic of prayer and worship is a form of prayer). Remember, **I Peter 2:9** says we are a *"...Royal Priesthood..."* Notice that David also said all things come from God and it is actually a privilege to be able to give back to Him.

Giving to God isn't something to be taken lightly. We shouldn't just throw our tithes and offerings in a basket during a service casually. It has to be consecrated. It must be an expression of love and gratitude for who God is and what he has done for us. When we give with this attitude and it is misused, those responsible will ultimately be accountable to God, but we will surely receive our blessing from him because we have done our part.

> *And God is able to make all grace (every favour and earthly blessing) come to you in abundance, so that you may always and under all circumstances and whatever the need be self-sufficient [possessing enough to require no aid or support and furnished in abundance for every good work and charitable donation].*
> I Corinthians 9:8

> *"While the earth remains, seedtime and harvest, cold and heat, summer and winter, and day and night shall not cease."*
> **Genesis 8:22**

There is definitely a rich reward for those who obey and serve God but the whole essence of worship is that, rewards alone shouldn't be the main motivator for our service. Instead, it must be our love for God.

In his letter to the church in Corinth, Paul encouraged them to ensure that their motives for serving God was right because whatever they claimed to be doing for the Lord would be tested and exposed for what it really was.

> *"The work of each [one] will become [plainly, openly] known (shown for what it is); for the day [of Christ] will disclose and declare it, because it will be revealed with fire, and the fire will test and critically appraise the character and worth of the work each person has done. If the works which any person has built on this Foundation [any product of his efforts whatever] survives [this test], he will get his reward. But if any person's work is burned up [under the test], he will suffer the loss [of it all, losing his reward], though he himself will be saved, but only as [one who has passed] through fire."* **I Corinthians 3:13-15**

It is worth taking a pause every now and then to ask ourselves whether we're doing what we do for the right reasons. Are our private lives consistent with what we show off in public? For the worship leader, are you really interested in leading God's people into his presence and seeing his glory revealed or you just want to show off your musical skills for all to see?

The fallow grounds of our hearts must be broken up and the altars of our lives must be rebuilt again for God to come and rain righteousness upon our lives. God must come again to reign supreme in our lives.

> *"Sow to yourselves according to righteousness (uprightness and right standing with God); reap according to mercy and loving-kindness. Break up your uncultivated ground, for it is time to seek the Lord, to inquire for and of Him, and to require His favour, till He comes and teaches you righteousness and rains His righteous gift of salvation upon you."* **Hosea 10:12**

Ultimately, the motives of our hearts will be the judge in our service to God and that is what true worship is all about.

The test of true worship is measured by the condition of our hearts. As we have seen throughout this book, there are scripturally prescribed ways to express this heart condition. However, for the expression to be a worthy sacrifice acceptable to the Lord, it has got to come from the right heart.

That is why the bible admonishes us to guard our hearts with all diligence since everything flows from it [Proverbs 4:23]. The *heart* is the seat of our motives, affections and desires.

Joel's prophesy to the nation of Israel in preparation for the impending revival pleaded with them to *"Rend their **hearts** and not their garments."* **Joel 2:13a**

Jesus said of the Pharisees that they honoured him with their lips but their **hearts** were far from Him [Matthew 15:8].

Again, Jesus said that *"Where your treasure is, there your **heart** will be also."* **Matthew 6:21**

The question is; how do we cultivate this heart condition? King David gives us a clue in this Psalm:

> *"Search me [thoroughly], O God, and know my heart! Try me and know my thoughts! And see if there is any wicked or hurtful way in me, and lead me in the way everlasting."* **Psalm 139:23-24**

For God to search and try us thoroughly, he will expose our true heart condition by the way we react to various unpleasant circumstances that come our way. We then have the option to either ask for his grace to enable us to walk in his ways or to persist in what we know is not his will.

The more we choose to walk in his ways in spite of the circumstances, the more our motives are purified and hence a worshiper's heart is created in us. The implication is that, the altar we are building will never be broken and ultimately, God will always be pleased with any sacrifice coming from that altar.

The choice is ours; will we rebuild the broken altars or do we want to leave them in ruins?

When we embrace this concept of worship; the total surrender and the giving away of ourselves unreservedly to God and not just the 30 minutes spent in worship expression during a church service, then we can expect God to reveal himself to us and use us for his glory.

Worship Nuggets

- A worship song becomes a sacrifice of worship to the Lord when it is a reflection of the singer's lifestyle or it is a heartfelt prayer to God.
- When singing a song of worship, our focus must be on the God we're singing to and not the song in itself.
- The quality of our lifestyle and character determines the potency of our worship expression.
- In true worship expression with our lips, the utterances must be coming from our hearts through our lips and not just mere lip service.
- The level of God's manifest presence we experience in our public gatherings is a reflection of our personal intimacy level with Him in private.
- The character of the vessel rendering worship determines the substance of the offering.
- The more we learn to 'practice' the omnipresence of God, the greater we'll experience the manifest presence of God.
- It is possible to sing a worship song without it coming from the heart but it is impossible to truly express our worship to God in song without it coming from the heart.
- When we truly worship in his Name, God will reveal the aspect of his Name that we need to experience in our lives.
- Worship in not an event; It is a lifestyle.
- Worship doesn't begin with a song! It begins with a heart condition.

About the Author

○ ○ ○

Douglas is passionate about the ministry of music and worship. Before relocating to the United Kingdom, he served in various capacities including worship leading for over 15 years at his local church in Ghana.

He is a professional web developer and has expertise in Front-End development, Microsoft SharePoint Administration and WordPress Installation and development.

Besides his passion for God and his Kingdom, his other interests include entrepreneurship, technology, blogging and sports.

He fellowships at Kingsway International Christian Centre (KICC), London, where he is a member.

Douglas currently lives in the United Kingdom with his wife, Julia.

○ ○ ○

www.ingramcontent.com/pod-product-compliance
Lightning Source LLC
Chambersburg PA
CBHW071839290426
44109CB00017B/1861